Wicca for Beginners

The ultimate guide to Wicca, Wiccan spells, Wiccan beliefs, rituals, magic, and witchcraft!

Table Of Contents

Introduction 1

Chapter 1: Wiccan History and Beliefs............................... 2

Chapter 2: The Law of Threefold Return and the Ethics of Magick 6

Chapter 3: Curses, Hexes, and Love Spells 9

Chapter 4: The Book of Shadows 12

Chapter 5: How to Cast a Spell 16

Chapter 6: Performing a Ritual 19

Chapter 7: Wiccan Deities 23

Chapter 8: Wicca Myths 29

Chapter 9: Different Tools Used in Wicca 31

Chapter 10: Finding a Coven 36

Chapter 11: Spells for Love 39

Chapter 12: Spells for Money 46

Chapter 13: Spells for Success 53

Chapter 14: Spells for Happiness 56

Chapter 15: Spells for Healing 59

Conclusion 62

Introduction

I want to thank you and congratulate you for picking up the book, "Wicca for Beginners".

This is the recently updated 2nd edition of this title. It has been updated with a range of new information, and great spells for the beginner to try! This can now be considered as a complete guide to Wicca, perfect for beginners!

This book contains helpful information about Wicca, what it is, and how you can become involved.

You will learn about the history of Wicca, including the common beliefs that Wiccans hold, who they worship, and how their magick works.

You will discover the facts about Wicca, and will have many myths dispelled. You will soon see the power that Wiccan magick holds, and how it is primarily used for good.

You'll also learn about the different uses and practices of Wicca, including different spells, rituals, and ceremonies. You will be provided with a range of different spells to try, for things like money, love, happiness, and success!

This book will help you to successfully understand and begin using these Wiccan spells today!

Whether you're a complete skeptic, or have a strong belief in Wiccan magick, this book will have something to offer you!

Thanks again for taking the time to read this book, I hope you enjoy it!

Chapter 1:
Wiccan History and Beliefs

The practice of the Wiccan religion began during the late 1940s to 1950s. Around this time, practitioners published numerous books and manuscripts on the subjects of witchcraft and Wicca. Even though Wicca as a religion is new, witchcraft has been around for thousands of years.

Since the early centuries, people regarded witchcraft as works of evil. They believed that witches were devil worshippers whose only mission was to make other people suffer. Because of such beliefs, Wicca gained a bad reputation amongst people of other religions. However, Wicca is actually a very peaceful and harmonious religion that aims to bring balance to life and promotes unity with the divine.

Wicca is all about appreciating the sun, moon, and stars. It is about respecting nature and everything in it. It is a belief system based upon the reconstruction of certain pre-Christian traditions in Wales, Ireland, and Scotland. Becoming a witch does not necessarily mean you will become evil. Instead, you will be a teacher, healer, giver, seeker, and protector of all things.

Gods of the Four Elements

Wiccans believe that gods and goddesses watch over people and nature, and each one of them serves his or her own purpose and destiny. When performing a ritual, it is crucial to call onto the four elements: fire, earth, water, and air. Keep in mind that energy can greatly influence your magick. While you can call upon any god and goddess that you want, you may want to request the presence of the gods and goddesses of the four elements to assist you in your magickal workings.

Lugh is the god of fire. He has the power of change and is represented by the color red. He brings power and energy when you need them for healing. Dana is the goddess of the earth. She possesses powers for realism and grounding. She is represented by the green, black, and dark brown colors. She will bring you the powers you need for prosperity and growth.

Cerredwen is the goddess of fluid transformation and water. Practitioners usually call upon her for friendship, metamorphosis, and peace. She is represented by the color blue and will provide you with the powers you need for change. Dagha is the god of air. He possesses the powers of thoughtfulness, wisdom, and intelligence by virtue of clarity. Call upon him for viable sensibilities and sound reasoning. He is represented by the colors yellow, light blue, and white.

Initiation and Degree Systems

Before you can become part of a coven, you have to undergo an initiation from a High Priestess or Priest. However, if you do not wish to be part of a coven, you can perform a self-dedication ritual to pledge yourself to the gods and goddesses.

For Wiccans, initiation symbolizes rebirth. Once initiated, you become dedicated to the gods and goddesses. Usually, only someone who reached the ranking of Third Degree dedicant can become a High Priestess or High Priest. If you want to advance to the next level, you need to study Wicca for one year and one day.

Wiccan Magick and the Spirit World

For Wiccans, magick is not supernatural, but rather a tool or skill set. They use a variety of tools when performing rituals and spells, such as wands, athame, herbs, candles, and crystals. They cast a sacred circle and call upon the gods and goddesses for assistance. Magick is harnessing and using subtle energies to produce positive results.

In many branches of Wicca, the concept of afterlife is a common subject. In fact, Wiccans are open to interactions with spirits and the unknown. They use runes, astrology, and tarot cards to find answers to certain questions. Nonetheless, not all Wiccans attempt to communicate with the dead.

Basic Wiccan Beliefs

Wiccans do not believe in heaven, hell, sin, confession, or the devil. Therefore, they cannot possibly be Satanists. They do not even require members to wear a certain type of clothing when performing rituals. While each coven has specific traditions, the core beliefs of Wicca remain the same.

In Wicca, nature requires respect and honor because the Divine dwells in it. Everything, from plants and animals to rocks and trees, are sacred elements. Wiccans are generally passionate about the environment. They also believe in the afterlife and karma. They believe that what they do in this lifetime can affect their next life.

Wiccans follow the Law of Threefold Return, and they use a Book of Shadows to perform spells, both of which you will learn about later on. They honor the male and female polarities of the Divine, which is present in all living creatures. Also, they speak about their ancestors with great honor because they believe that they are always watching over them.

Wiccans celebrate eight major Sabbats annually and Esbats monthly. These holidays are based on the cycle of the seasons and turning of the Earth. Wiccans take responsibility for their actions. They can do anything they want as long as they do not harm anyone, as stated in their creed the Wiccan Rede.

Moreover, Wiccans respect the religious beliefs of other people. They do not recruit, preach, or convert people outside of their religion.

Chapter 2:
The Law of Threefold Return and the Ethics of Magick

As mentioned earlier, Wiccans believe in the Law of Threefold Return. They believe that whatever they do to others will come back to them threefold. So if they performed magick with the intention of hurting someone, the universe will make sure that they receive the same treatment, but three times worse. This is why the elders warn members against doing harm to others.

The Law of Threefold Return is actually a caveat given to witches, especially Neo-Wiccan ones, who have just been initiated. Its main purpose is to provide caution against performing negative magick. It reminds new witches that they do not have magical super powers, which is why they should not perform any spells without thinking about the consequences thoroughly.

An early incantation of this rule is in the High Magic's Aid, a novel written by Gerald Gardner. Gerald Gardner, also known as Scire, was a Wiccan anthropologist, archaeologist, and author. He contributed much to the publicity of the Contemporary Pagan religion and even wrote several of its definitive religious texts. He was also the founder of Gardnerian Wicca, one of the prominent Wiccan groups.

Later on, the Law of Threefold Return appeared in the form of poem in a magazine. Eventually, new witches adopted the notion that a spiritual law affects everything they do, negative or positive. The Law of Threefold Return is actually not an ugly concept, especially if you only focus on doing good things. If you do bad things to other people, expect bad things to happen to you as well.

Are there any objections to the Law of Threefold Return? Well, in order for a law to be regarded as a law, it has to be universal. This means that it has to apply to every person at all times. However, not all bad deeds receive punishment and not all good deeds are rewarded. In fact, some witches have admitted to doing harmful magick and not suffering from any bad consequences afterwards.

Anyway, there is another theory with regard to the Law of Threefold Return. Some witches believe that whatever you do in your current lifetime will happen again in your next lifetime but with three times more intensity. So if you have been a good person in this lifetime, you will have a good life when you get reincarnated after you die. Likewise, if you have been a bad person, you will likely suffer in your next life.

On the other hand, certain covens use the Law of Threefold Return as a means to give back what they have received. So when they received something positive, they give it back threefold. Similarly, when they received something negative, they can give it back threefold as well. You should take note that only members initiated into upper degree levels can, and are allowed to do this.

Ethics of Magick

In Wicca, there is a saying that black magick refers to magick that works while white magick is the opposite. As a beginner, you may get confused with these two types of magick, since pop culture, including television shows and movies, has taught you that black magick is evil. However, this is not exactly the case.

A lot of people associate black magick with darkness and white magick with light. Nonetheless, darkness does not really equate to evil. It simply represents what lies beneath the earth, long winter nights, or death. Once you are able to accept that darkness is not bad, it will be much easier for you to view the concept of white magick and black magick as the same thing.

Magick can only be harmful if you intend it to be. Keep in mind that your intent can be just as powerful as your actions. Magick is simply a tool you can use for whatever purpose you have. Think of it this way: magick is like a hammer that you can either use to build houses or hurt people. The hammer itself is not bad. It will only be bad if you use it to hurt people instead of building houses.

The same thing goes with magick. Regardless if it is black magick or white magick, it will only be negative if you use it for things that have a negative outcome. But how about casting spells, hexes, and curses? Is it ethical to cast a negative spell against someone if it benefits the majority? Is it alright to cast a love spell? These topics will be covered in the next chapter.

Chapter 3:
Curses, Hexes, and Love Spells

Some Wiccan groups believe that performing magick in order to achieve personal gain is wrong. They stick to this belief regardless of whether the magick is harmful to any other person or not. However, some groups believe otherwise. They allow their members to perform magick in order to improve their quality of life, find a lover, or do better at work as long as it only affects the spell caster and no one else.

So, you can use magick to improve your life and make you more comfortable. You can even use it to help other people but only with their consent. There is nothing wrong with using magick to gain a substantial amount of wealth, find love, or get rid of your woes. You can actually rely on magick to help you grow and empower yourself. You can use it to fulfill your desires, ambitions, and dreams.

Now, what about hexes and curses? Is it okay to bind, hex, curse, or cast a negative spell against another person if your intention is pure and good? Well, this has a case-to-case basis. If you are part of a group or coven that allows it, then you may do so. Dianic Witches, for instance, allow hexing, cursing, binding, and other negative forms of magick on those who have harmed women.

Such witches believe that cursing and hexing are applicable to people who have harmed others. They believe that such actions are allowable if their intention is for the common good. For instance, they may curse or hex a criminal in order to stop them from committing any more crimes. Even though the action is negative, the intent is positive. Hence, it can be an exemption to the rule of not harming anyone.

Similarly, there are witches who allow negative magick as a form of self-defense. If someone attacks you, for instance, you can curse or hex your attacker. Just make sure that you perform magick wisely and carefully. Think of your spells thoroughly and do not let your emotions take control. On the other hand, if you do not feel comfortable with such negative magick, you should avoid practicing it altogether.

What about a love spell? Can you cast a spell to make someone fall in love with you? Well, technically the answer is yes. However, doing so would be a violation of the rule. If you aim your love spell at a specific target, you will be violating the freedom of that person. Manipulating or taking away the free will of others is taboo and considered as negative magick.

If you wish to cast a love spell, you should just focus on yourself. Instead of trying to force a specific person to love you, you should ask the powers of the universe to help you improve yourself so you can attract the right kind of person or be more likeable. You can also use magick to help you increase your self-esteem. You may be having a hard time finding a suitable partner because of your insecurities or lack of confidence.

In this case, you need to cast a spell that will let you have a positive makeover. You can cast a generic love spell that does not interfere with the free will of anyone else. You can cast a love spell that can help you become more noticeable or attractive in the eyes of the opposite sex. You can also use a love spell that will enable your object of affection to see all your positive qualities.

Keep in mind that it is not ethical to use magick on someone without their knowledge or consent. It is not ethical to try to destroy the relationship of other people either. Unfortunately, there are people who are so desperate that they want to break up a marriage or relationship in order to obtain the attention of the attached person they are attracted to. Don't fall into this trap, and remember to only use magick when it's ethical to do so.

Chapter 4:
The Book of Shadows

The Book of Shadows is one of the most important things that you can have as a witch or Wiccan. It is a sacred tool and therefore requires consecration along with the other tools on your altar. It contains vital information that you have to understand and learn by heart. You can copy rituals and spells by hand or have them computerized. Most Wiccan traditions advise their members to have their Book of Shadows handwritten.

You can also make your own Book of Shadows. You should feel free to modify spells or create your own. When creating your very own Book of Shadows, you should start with an empty book or notebook. You can also get blank pages and simply bind them together. See to it that your Book of Shadows is made of sturdy materials so it will not get damaged easily.

Use sheet protectors to protect the pages against candle wax and drippings. Do not forget to write your name on the title page. You can make it simple or fancy, it's all up to you. As for the contents, you can write anything you want. You can also use the language that you are most comfortable using. However, there are certain sections that you need to include.

For instance, you have to write down the laws of your group or coven. Different Wiccan groups have different rules you have to abide by. If you belong to a particular group, copy the rules from their Book of Shadows. Some of the most popular groups are Alexandrian, Blue Star, British Traditional, Circle Sanctuary, Covenant of the Goddess, Dianic, Eclectic, Gardnerian, and Seax Wicca.

However, if you are a solitary practitioner or your group does not have any written rules or guidelines, you can write down rules that you believe are acceptable and reasonable. It is important for you to set boundaries, so you do not cross the line. As a witch, you have to be disciplined and responsible. You can include the Wiccan Rede and other similar concepts in your Book of Shadows.

If you belong to a group or coven, you may also include a copy of your initiation ceremony. You can also write down whose god or goddess you are dedicating yourself to. You can even include the reason why you chose that particular deity. Feel free to use as many pages as you want. Your dedication can be a short paragraph or a lengthy essay.

In Wicca, there are numerous gods and goddesses involved. So depending on what group or coven you belong to, you may choose a specific god or goddess. Make sure that you reserve a space in your Book of Shadows for the myths, legends, and artwork associated with your chosen deity. If you are following an eclectic path, you can elaborate your faith in this book.

Do not forget to include correspondence tables that feature herbs, crystals, stones, colors, and moon phases. These correspondence tables are highly crucial in spell-casting. Take note that certain spells are best casted on specific moon phases. If you want your spell to work, you also have to use the right herbs, crystals, or stones. Write down important information with regard to these elements in your Book of Shadows.

If you are not that knowledgeable when it comes to herbs, you can ask for assistance from experienced witches. As a beginner, you have to pay attention to the history and properties of these herbs. You also have to find out if they can be ingested or applied topically. Herbalism is actually very important in spell-casting. Plants are crucial ingredients in potions, etc.

Likewise, you should have a space for magickal recipes that involve herbs, oils, and other elements. You can collect recipes from books or even online. Write down recipes that you think are useful for your practice. Also, you should take note of the tools and equipment that are necessary. Such recipes are especially useful when celebrating Sabbats.

In Wicca, the Wheel of the Year consists of eight major Sabbats, namely Samhain, Imbolc or Imbolg, Yule, Ostara, Litha, Beltane, Mabon, and Lughnasadh or Lammas. Some traditions, however, only celebrate some of these holidays. Nonetheless, you should make sure that you write about the Sabbats in your Book of Shadows. Take note of their dates, rituals, and other crucial aspects.

If you want to celebrate every full moon, you may also include an Esbat rite in your Book of Shadows. You can use the same rite every time or use a different one every month. You may even write down information regarding Drawing Down the Moon, casting a circle, or any other rites for prosperity, healing, and protection. Drawing Down the Moon is a rite that celebrates the invoking of the goddess during the full moon.

If you are interested in scrying, Tarot, astrology, and other forms of divination, you should also write about them in your Book of Shadows. Make sure that you write down what you did and what results you have acquired. Likewise, be sure to allot a space for sacred texts in your Book of Shadows. You can include old prayers in archaic languages, chants, or The Charge of the Goddess.

As for your spells, you may write them down in your Book of Shadows or keep them in a grimoire. If you do not want to use a separate book for your spells, you can simply write them down in your Book of Shadows. Just make sure that you categorize them according to purpose. You can write down spells for protection, prosperity, and healing among others.

Aside from keeping them organized, you should include more information such as the outcome of each spell. This is particularly helpful if you are the one who wrote the spells. By taking notes of their results, you will know which spells work and which ones do not. This way, you can stick to the spells that work and modify the ones that do not yield your desired outcomes.

Remember that your Book of Shadows is sacred. Hence, you need to make sure that you take care of it properly, and keep it constantly updated. You can use ring binders so it will be easier to insert additional pages. Handle it with utmost care and use dividers to keep the pages organized. Do not forget to include a table of contents or an index for greater ease of use.

Chapter 5:
How to Cast a Spell

As a beginner, it is perfectly acceptable for you to use the spells of other people. You can copy a spell from a book or get one online. There are actually a lot of free spells available today. Over time, however, you should learn to write your own spells. Using your original material will make you feel more comfortable and confident with the outcome.

When writing a spell, make sure that you have a clear intention or goal, identify what it is that you want to accomplish. Perhaps, you want achieve financial stability or prosperity, or you are looking for love or seeking a partner. You may also want to improve yourself by boosting your confidence or self-esteem, or you may want to improve your health. Whatever it is that you want to accomplish, you have to be very clear about it.

Once you've determined your goal or desired outcome, gather the necessary materials you will need for the ritual. You may need candles, herbs, crystals, and stones. Keep in mind that magick is mostly about symbolism. Hence, you need to find the elements or materials that symbolize your desire.

For instance, if you want to attract love, use a red candle since the color symbolizes love. If you want to have more money, you can light a green candle or use a jade gemstone because the color green and jade tend to represent money. You can also use unusual items, such as toys, accessories, decorative ornaments, or clothing. You can use anything you want as long as they are symbolic.

Timing is also of great importance. Some spells work best on certain days, hours, or moon phases. Love spells and other positive spells, for instance, are best done during nights of the waxing moon. On the other hand, binding spells and other negative spells are advisable during nights of the waning moon. Many witches also believe that Friday is a strong day for spells.

Then again, it is still up to you to choose the date and time for your spells. If you are using the spell of someone else and that spell requires you to perform it at a certain time but you cannot make it, do not feel discouraged. You can still perform the spell at a time that is convenient for you. You should not feel obligated to immerse yourself in details. If you are confident in your magickal abilities, your spells will work no matter what date and time you cast them.

Nonetheless, see to it that you are very careful about the words and phrases you use for your spells. The universe can be very tricky, which is why you need to put a lot of thought into your wordings. If you want to chant, come up with good, yet sensible rhymes. Make sure that your spells are clear and specific. Remember that once you have uttered them, you can no longer take them back unless you redo the spell.

So how long can you expect your spell to manifest? The exact time varies depending on your spell. Some spells take effect immediately or within hours, while some will take days, weeks, or months to manifest. According to certain traditions, you may redo your spell if you do not see any results within twenty-eight days. Find out which variables you may have to change in order for the spell to work.

Is there a possibility that your spell will not work? Well, your spells may not work if you were unclear, your intentions were bad, or you have doubts with your spell-work. You may also fail to see results if you do not fully release your spell. Hence, you should refrain from constantly worrying or obsessing about your spell. Once you cast it, let go and allow the universe to do the rest.

Chapter 6:
Performing a Ritual

Rituals play a huge part in the Wiccan religion. When performing a ritual, you have to make sure that you have the right tools. An altar, for instance, is essential. It is a focal point that contains all the tools that you may need during the ritual. Your altar can be simple or elaborate. It can be made of any material, but wood is preferable. You can decorate it with ornaments, cloth, or jewelry.

You do not necessarily have to have every single tool associated with Wicca. An athame or sword, for instance, may not be needed if you are performing a simple love spell. Nonetheless, this small knife may be necessary if you are performing a rite for a Sabbat. The same rule applies with the boline, another kind of knife. If you do not need to cut anything during your ritual then you can make do without the boline.

Some of the most common tools used by witches during rituals include wands, besoms, chalices, bells, cauldrons, sensors, crystal balls, and tiles. While witches or Wiccans are not exactly required to wear a specific kind of clothing, you may want to wear something that is comfortable such as a robe with flared sleeves and a hood. If you do not have a robe, your casual clothes are fine.

On the other hand, if you prefer to perform your rituals in the nude, you may do so. Some witches actually perform rituals naked, although most are solitary practitioners. As for your jewelry and accessories, you can wear a necklace, ring, or bracelet that features a symbolic gemstone or even your birthstone. You can also wear an amulet or a celestial symbol if you want.

Anyway, see to it that your altar is ready before you begin your ritual. When everything is ready, you can begin. Make sure that you complete each step in the right order. As a beginner, you should write down the ritual steps as well as your spells on a piece of paper to serve as a guide. You can also write down the names of the deity you wish to call upon.

Steps of a Ritual

First of all, you must cast a circle to open up the portal. When casting a circle, you can use your wand or finger to draw a circle, or simply walk around in a circle; just make sure that you draw the circle clockwise, three times, and starting from the north. Keep your mind focused on drawing your circle and imagine the energies swirling surrounding you.

After drawing your circle, you have to state your purpose. As much as possible, you should speak loud and clear to ensure that the gods and goddesses hear you. Ideally, you should perform one ritual per request. However, if you wish to request for more than one thing, you may do so as well. You can write them down on a piece of paper so you will not forget them.

Once you have stated your purpose, call upon your chosen deity. You can actually call upon a variety of gods and goddesses from different traditions. You can seek assistance from Greek, Celtic, Norse, and Egyptian deities. Make sure that you invoke the presence of the right god or goddess. For instance, if you are casting a love spell, you should call upon Aphrodite or Venus.

It would also be helpful to have some sort of offering to the gods and goddesses. In general, wine, bread, and milk are valid offerings. Nonetheless, you may choose to offer something specific if you are requesting the presence of a particular god or goddess. If you are invoking Aphrodite, you may offer roses. If you are invoking Cato for agricultural prosperity, you may offer wheat, lard, and meat.

Likewise, you may offer lavender and honey to other gods and goddesses of love and passion. If you are invoking a god or goddess of prosperity and abundance, you can offer beer, catnip, grains, and dairy. If you need help from a goddess of fertility and childbirth, you can offer eggs, apple bosoms, and baked goods. If you are calling upon a god or goddess of the hearth and home, you can offer cider and thyme.

During the invocation of the deities, you should request their presence or ask them to enter your body. You may also request to communicate with them in the form of an apparition or vision. Throughout this step, see to it that you focus all of your energy. Prevent your mind from wandering off.

After the offerings is the time to perform magick. Performing magick is a major part of any ritual. It is during this time that you cast your spells or ask the deity a special favor. See to it that you provide every crucial bit of information; be as detailed as possible. Once you state your request, do not forget to thank the deity and give your offerings.

Finally, you have to close the circle to seal the portal. Just as you have done when you cast the circle, you can use your wand or finger to trace the circle in a counter-clockwise direction. You can also walk around counter-clockwise three times. Closing the circle is a very important step. You need to free up the energies and the deities that you have called upon during your ritual.

Chapter 7:
Wiccan Deities

For Wiccans, the Divine is manifested through the God and the Goddess. Neither one is greater than the other. Because of our human limitations, perceiving the Divine through masculine and feminine sides make it easier for us to grasp and relate with the concept of the Divine energy. Simply put, when attuning themselves with nature and with the creative powers of the universe, Wiccans (whether covens or solo practitioners) follow whichever practices they are most comfortable with. That's the beauty of Wiccan religion. You get to choose your deities. Though sometimes, it's the divine being that chooses you.

When practicing spells and rituals, Wiccans tend to call the Divine by different names. However, this doesn't mean that they are addressing separate deities. They are, in fact, addressing the various aspects of the Divine. These aspects come together to form the One. When beseeching the aid of Wiccan goddesses in a ritual, you will notice that several names may be used by some practitioners. These are actually titles which do not necessarily always refer to several different goddesses. Nor do these titles exclusively belong to one goddess in particular.

For instance, the title Queen of Heaven may be used to refer to, but is not exclusive to, Asherah or the Virgin Mary or any other Mother Goddesses such as Isis, Gaia, Parvati, etc. The title Triple Goddess is used to refer to the three aspects of the Goddess: Maiden, Mother, and Crone. In India, the title Triple Goddess is used to address Kali. In Ireland, it is used to address Brighid. For the Greeks, it may be the three Gorgons, the three Moerae, or Hebe, Hera, and Hecate. To the Druids, the Triple Goddess is Diana Triformis.

Despite the differences in deity names and worship practices among various Wiccan groups, here are a few basic concepts which most of them agree upon:

The existence of the One

The One is the supreme creative power. It existed even before the beginning of the Earth, in knowing, in silence, in stillness, and in solitude. It is that which unites everything which exists in the universe. The One is all-encompassing. The One is infinite.

The One is manifested through masculine and feminine forces in nature

The God (also called the Lord) and the Goddess (also called the Lady) signifies the polarities of the One. When brought together, these masculine and feminine energies form an omnipresent energy which makes creation possible. The feminine and the masculine characteristics of the One serve to complement each other, bringing about harmony in the universe.

There are some Wiccan traditions that prefer to worship specific deities instead of honoring a single all-encompassing divinity. Here are some of the Wiccan gods and goddesses which have found their way into even contemporary Wiccan traditions.

Popular Celtic Deities

Brighid

She is the goddess of the hearth, fertility, the feminine arts, and occult wisdom. She is the patron of poets, healers, and magicians. Wiccans in the Celtic tradition seek her guidance in matters relating to clairvoyance.

Honoring Brighid is best done during Imbolc through a group ceremony around a fire. You may also honor her by making and offering handicrafts such as a corn doll fashioned in the image of the Goddess Brighid, a bride's bed for the Goddess, or the Brighid's cross.

The Dagda

The "good god" is a powerful Father deity is represented as a great man with a large phallus wielding a giant club. This club possesses the power to end the lives of men or to resurrect them. Also in his possession is a cauldron of enormous size, bearing endless supplies of sustenance. He is the god of fertility. He is also the god of knowledge.

Cailleach

Whereas Brighid rules the months of summer, Cailleach is the queen of the darker half of the year. She rules from Samhain to Beltane. This means that it is best to honor her or seek her assistance during these months. Cailleach is depicted as an old woman riding the back of a wolf, wielding a hammer made of human flesh. She has the power to destroy and to create life. She is the protector of wild animals.

To honor her, adorn your home with apples and gourds. Use obsidian, deadly nightshade, sage, or catnip in your spells.

Ceridwen

She is the goddess of magick, herbs, spells, and inspiration which makes her very important to practicing Wiccans. In Wales, they celebrate the Festival of Ceridwen in July.

Morrighan

She is the goddess of war. In the olden times, it was she who determined whether one lives or dies on the battlefield. Morrighan governs night magick and prophecy. She is the patroness of witches.

Popular Greek Deities

Eros

He is the Greek god of fertility and sexuality and thus, you may call upon his aid when performing a love spell or a spell for passion.

Aphrodite

Known as the goddess of love and beauty, Wiccans call upon her when performing love rituals or spells to enhance one's physical qualities.

Hecate

She is the goddess of magick and sorcery. Modern Wiccans call upon her as the "Dark Goddess" due to her connection with the spirit world. She governs the dark moon. That said, Hecate is not a deity whom you would wish to invoke lightly.

Bacchus/ Dionysus

He is the god of ritual ecstasy. Though popularly known as the god of wine, you may also seek his help in agriculture or in matters of communication between the dead and the living. Honor him in groups in the woods by drinking wine and singing hymns to his name while being one with nature.

Popular Wiccan Gods from Other Cultures

Shiva

He is the Hindu god responsible for destroying obstacles and aiding in transformation.

Thoth

In Egyptian culture, he is the god of magick and wisdom.

Odin

In Norse tradition, he is regarded as the Father God. Wiccans call upon him when they wish to gain wealth, wisdom, and aid in prophecy.

Popular Wiccan Goddesses from Other Cultures

Isis

The Egyptian Mother Goddess is the matriarch of nature and the matron of magick.

Maya

In Hindu tradition, she is the goddess of mystery and illusion.

Shekina

In Hebrew tradition, she is the goddess of compassion.

Inanna

From Sumerian history, she is believed to be the goddess of sexual love and fertility.

Frigg

She is the Norse goddess of the home. Seek her help when performing rituals for a lasting and happy marriage.

Chapter 8:
Wicca Myths

The goal of this chapter is to address and clarify popular myths surrounding Wiccan practice.

- First of all, Wicca is not a new age fad. It is a religion that has been around for centuries. Though the medieval church employed massive efforts in order to destroy written records of Wiccan faith, archaeologists were able to discover proof that can be traced back to the Paleolithic age when our predecessors worshipped the Goddess of Fertility and the God of the Hunt.

- Another common myth is that Wicca is evil. On the contrary, the Wiccan belief system promotes a non-violent approach to life. *"An Ye Harm None, Do What Ye Will"*. Such is the Wiccan creed. Though rules may differ from coven to coven, this is the generally agreed-upon creed. You can do whatever it is that you're supposed to do as long as it does not hurt or endanger anyone. While it's true that one cannot control a person's intentions, Wiccans are discouraged from using their knowledge of magick to harm others. To be Wiccan is to co-exist in harmony with all beings and powers in this universe.

- Wiccan religion is not unregulated. When joining Wiccan covens, there are initiations and degrees. The latter is used to describe the member's stages of learning. Apart from the Wiccan creed, almost all Wiccan groups believe in the Rule of Threefold Return. That is, whatever energy you send out there, be it positive or negative, will return to you three times in strength.

- Wicca does not involve demon worship. The difference between other religions and the Wiccan belief system is that the latter does not recognize the existence of a superlative evil. While certain religions may use the concept of eternal damnation to frighten their followers into obedience, Wiccans are encouraged to exist in love and harmony with other beings simply because it is the right thing to do.

Some people mistakenly think that Wiccans worship the devil because of the use of the pentacle during rituals. Contrary to what pop culture has made people believe, there's nothing evil about the pentacle. For Wiccans, the five-pointed star represents the five elements: air, water, fire, earth, and spirit.

Chapter 9:
Different Tools Used in Wicca

Every beginner should be made familiar with the basic tools used in Wiccan spells and rituals, as well as with the meaning behind the different tools. Some of these tools are man-made while others can be obtained from nature.

Natural tools may be used in rituals to represent a particular element. That said, there is one rule that a practicing Wiccan should know before harvesting tools from nature: "Take only that which is willing." You will know whether an animate object such as a crystal (yes, crystals possess life!) or a tree is willing to sacrifice themselves for your spells if you feel no sense of heaviness or resistance when you touch them.

Usually, when an object is cool to touch, that signals "No". On the other hand, if it radiates warmth, it means that it is willing to participate in your spell/ritual.

Common Natural Wiccan Tools

Stones and Crystals

Symbolizing Earth and the North, they are commonly used for healing or as foundations or offerings for altars. Crystals emit vibrations which can be used for physical, emotional, and spiritual healing, and for assisting one to connect with his/her higher self. There are also crystals which awaken a person's clairvoyant abilities.

Herbs

Symbolic of the Earth Spirit and the North, they are often required in Wiccan spells.

Shells

Symbolizing the Water Spirit and the West, they are often used to contain energy.

Feathers

Symbolizing the Air Spirit and the East, they are used to purify energies.

Sticks

Symbolizing the Fire Spirit and the South, they may be utilized as instruments for dowsing or as materials for creating wands.

Other Common Wiccan Altar Tools

Candles

When used to invoke the powers of a direction, green, brown and black candles represent the North. Meanwhile, the East is represented by white or yellow candles. Blue candles are used to represent the West while red or orange ones are for the South. Gold, silver, or white candles are usually placed at the center of the altar.

When performing a spell, knowing the meaning behind the color of each candle will aid you in which one to use.

- White candles symbolize truth and purity.
- Red candles are often used in love spells as they signify sex, passion, and power.
- For money spells, green candles are recommended.

- Pink candles are best for spells involving love, friendship, and honor.

- Purple signifies ambition and success.

- Orange is commonly used for spells of attraction.

- Light blue candles may be used for spells for achieving health and peace.

- A brown candle symbolizes neutrality.

- Black candles symbolize negativity and confusion.

The Cauldron

This traditional Wiccan tool is commonly used for brewing potions. But more than that, it is symbolic of transformation. The cauldron also signifies the Goddess, as well as femininity and fertility. It is associated with the Water Spirit and is often the central point of Wiccan rituals.

The Chalice

This Wiccan tool is symbolic of the Goddess and also represents the Water Spirit. In a way, the chalice is similar to the cauldron. It is also used to mix potions in small amounts. For certain rituals, the chalice is used to hold saltwater which is needed to cleanse objects. Also, the chalice is used as a container for ritual wine.

The Besom

This is otherwise known as the broomstick. As awesome as the idea may seem, witches never really used the besom for flight. However, they did use the besom to aid them in astral projection (out of the body experiences). The besom is also utilized to sweep away (symbolically, not physically) negative energies prior to performing rituals and after conducting them.

The Athame

Though this Wiccan tool is indeed a knife, it is intentionally fashioned to be dull and it commonly has a double edge. Its purpose is not for cutting. Instead, it is used to direct energies when performing rituals. Some athames have magickal symbols carved into them. Because this tool resembles a phallus, it represents the God or the Lord. It is associated with the Fire Spirit.

The Boline

This knife is one which you can actually use for cutting. You may use it during or outside rituals. Among its many purposes are for cutting herbs, fashioning wands, and engraving symbols.

The Censer

This Wiccan ceremonial tool is used as a container for incense which is a popular ingredient for spells and rituals. In the absence of a censer, a plain bowl may be used. The Censer is associated with the Spirit of Air.

The Book of Shadows

The Book of Shadows refers to the Wiccan's workbook. This is where you keep your personal spells and your notes. A Book of Shadows may be something that you've created, or the book and the knowledge within it may have been passed down from one generation to another. Some contemporary Wiccans store their spells in a laptop or any other device, but you should know that during the act of writing, energy is transferred from you to the paper. This adds to the effectiveness of the spells.

Chapter 10:
Finding a Coven

There are many advantages to joining a coven as opposed to being a solo practitioner. For one thing, as a beginner, you will benefit greatly from the wisdom of other more experienced Wiccans. A coven's structured lesson plan makes it easier for novices in the Wiccan religion to grasp certain concepts. More than that, joining a group will enable you to widen your social network. Lastly, one of the most important benefits that a coven can provide you is support and protection.

It will be a bit more challenging for you find a coven in your area if you aren't ready to proclaim yourself as Wiccan. Likewise, Wiccan groups aren't necessarily keen on publicizing themselves. If you're still in the broom closet, so to speak, one of the ways in which you can discreetly attract the attention of fellow Wiccans is by wearing Wiccan jewelry. Nothing breaks the ice better than a cool pentacle pendant. Too obvious? Try wearing God/Goddess symbols. Hopefully, someone who is familiar with these symbols will strike up a conversation.

If you're bold, then your best bet would be to join Wiccan workshops. If this isn't a possibility for you, try hanging around alternative bookstores and local health food stores.

To increase your chances of stumbling upon fellow Wiccans, you may enroll in Tarot, Palmistry, Energy Healing, or Astrology classes. A lot of Wiccans also attend meditation classes.

If the strategies above fail to work, don't despair. There's always the presence of online communities where individuals more freely proclaim themselves as Wiccan. You may also find an index of covens and Pagan groups online.

Once you have found a coven, it's time to ask yourself the following questions:

- What are the coven's rules?

- Will I be able to abide by these rules?

- Are these rules in line with my principles?

Keep in mind that there are some Wiccan groups that are exclusive only to males or females. Some only accept singles while others are run by families.

Stay away from covens that…

- ask you to work for the High Priest or Priestess as a form of initiation. A coven is not a college fraternity/sorority.

- ask you to have sex with the High Priest or Priestess or any member/s of the group as part of the initiation. You may be told that the ritual is merely a symbolic union between the Lord and the Lady.

- ask strangers to join their group. Covens don't go out there recruiting new members. The beginner must ask to join the coven. It may take months for a novice to be admitted to a coven. After that, you must pass through several degrees of initiation. The learning phase usually involves years of study.

Keep in mind that rituals performed by groups are usually more complex and time-consuming. When joining a coven, prepare to arrange your schedule to fit your congregation's calendar of events. That said, Wiccan festivals are certainly more fun when celebrated with individuals who share and understand your beliefs.

Chapter 11:
Spells for Love

Love spells are perhaps the most sought-after Wiccan spells. And why not? It is in our nature to seek love and companionship. Before engaging in love spells, even in the most basic ones, it is necessary to clarify your intentions first. Are you hoping to find your soul mate? Are you already in love with someone and are wishing to be loved in return? Or are you looking for a way to rekindle the waning flame of an existing relationship? Each specific intention has a corresponding spell and it is necessary that you choose the correct one.

If you're looking to invite love into your life…

Perform the following love spell during the week after the New Moon.

- Cast a circle.

- Arrange three yellow candles in a triangular formation.

- Then, place a white candle in the middle of the triangle.

- Afterwards, scatter red rose petals around yourself.

- Call upon the Goddess of Love (Aphrodite or whichever deity you prefer) to bless the circle. (ex. "Goddess of Love, I call upon thee to fill this circle with your love and beauty.")

- Using your personally-written spell, ask for the Goddess to guide your soul mate so that he/she will find their way to you.

- Next, say these words: "Such is my will."

- Sip some tea from freshly brewed mint leaves.

- Then, snuff out the candles beginning with the white candle.

- Lastly, gather the rose petals and wrap them between sheets of paper. Leave the petals to dry for about a week.

- After the petals have dried, select a flowing body of water, such as a river. Then scatter the dried petals there.

- As the water carries away the energy of your intention, hope that your invitation finds its way to your soul mate.

If you already have a specific person in mind...

The following magick spell works by sending a beam of love energy toward the object of your affection which he/she will be able to feel subconsciously. The result is he/she will become more receptive to your affections. However, this spell draws power from white energy and so, it does not work by forcing someone to love you against their will (there are black magick spells that can do that but using them is highly discouraged). The advantage of this spell is that it purifies and strengthens the link between you and your beloved.

- Perform this spell at night.

- Cast a circle. Invite your chosen deity (ex. Eros or Aphrodite), to grace your circle.

- Light a fire inside a cauldron.

- Then using red-colored ink, draw a heart on a small piece of paper. Inscribe the person's name inside it.

- In your mind's eye, envision a ray of pink energy gushing forth from your heart and onto the piece of paper. Think of the heart on the paper as your beloved's heart. Send forth love energy from your heart to his/hers.

- Then, take the paper and kiss your beloved's name three times.

- Drop the piece of paper into the fire and allow the flames to consume it.

- Meanwhile, utter a personal spell stating how you are sending your love to that person and how you are hoping that he/she may find it in his/her heart to love you in return.

- After you're done reciting your incantation, say these words: "So mote it be."

- Then, close the circle. Do this by thanking the deity whose aid you have sought.

If you want to increase your lover's passion…

This spell may be done with or without your partner's consent. That said, it's up to you to gauge whether the spell needs to be discussed with your lover first. Keep in mind that with or without spells, honesty and open communication are necessary ingredients for successful marriages/relationships. Perform the following spell for three consecutive nights.

- Set four red candles in the east, west, north, and south. Then, set a white candle in the center.

- On the left side of the center candle, place some Ylang Ylang incense.

- Meanwhile, on the right side, place a bowl containing a Garnet crystal and three mint leaves.

- Then, set a photograph of your lover in front of the white candle.

- Cast the circle.

- Next, light the red candles, followed by the single white one, and lastly, the incense.

- Afterwards, pour some wax from the white candle onto the image of your partner.

- Take the bowl and in your mind's eye, see the circle glowing and brimming with red light, the same color as the Garnet. This symbolizes passion and sex drive. Continue doing this until you are able to sense the air thrumming with passionate energy.

- Then, recite an incantation calling the help of the Goddess of Love. Ask your deity to awaken the fire within your beloved and to revive his/her desire for you.

- Finally, snuff the flames from the candles and then close your circle, but not without thanking the Goddess first.

- Leave the Ylang Ylang to burn.

If you want to mend your relationship...

This spell is done to smooth things over after you and your lover have had an argument. While only you can truly resolve the fundamental issues in your relationship, this spell will make it easier for the both of you to get over something unpleasant that has transpired.

- Obtain a slender lavender candle and break it in half. However, be careful not to cut the wick. As a result, the candle is broken but both ends are still joined together by the wick.

- Concentrate on the problem that you would like to overcome. Focus on thinking up of ways for how you can solve it and how you intend on making it up to your partner.

- Using a handful of powdered basil, coat the broken edges of the lavender candle.

- Afterwards, firmly join the edges back together.

- Light a white candle. Then, pour some wax over the broken spot to mend it.

- When the lavender candle is whole once more, light it and allow it to burn until the flame reaches the part where the break used to be.

- Next, take a seat while holding the candle and concentrate on the fire as it makes its way down the formerly severed area. Meanwhile, think of your lover and think of ways how you can improve your relationship.

- After the flame has passed that crucial part, allow the candle to burn to the end.

If you wish to reunite with a former lover...

This spell is to be performed if you want to get back together with your ex. However, prior to doing this spell, be sure that you are devoid of any malicious intent. Do this only when you've tried but cannot bring yourself to love anyone else. Do this without plans of revenge in mind.

This spell, like all the others in this book, is fairly simple and perfect for beginners. However, what makes it a bit complicated is the fact that it can only be performed once a year on Midsummer's Eve. So this means you need to perform the spell on the *evening before* the longest day of the year (that's usually on June 20th or 21st).

- The first and perhaps the most difficult thing that you need to do is to find these three different locations:

- a tree which has a bird's nest

- a running body of water (ex. river, stream)

- a church

- a place where two roads cross

If you live in the city, this means that you're going to have to schedule a trip to a more rural location.

- After you've found these places, all you need to do is to bury one rose in each of these different locations.

- One of the roses should be buried beneath the tree. The other should be buried near the church's entryway. One rose is to be buried in the ground near the running body of water while the other is to be lain where two roads cross. Remember that this must all be done during Midsummer's Eve.

- Lastly, place a rose underneath your pillow. It should remain there for at least three consecutive nights.

- After three nights, take the rose and pluck its petals.

- Return to the four locations where you've buried the roses and scatter a few petals on those areas.

Chapter 12:
Spells for Money

Just like love spells, magick spells for money vary depending on one's intention. Some spells are performed to invite abundance into your life. Others are done to increase an existing fortune. Meanwhile, there are spells that may be performed to enhance your luck before starting a venture that could potentially generate money. Be warned though that the following spells are not substitutes to employment or hard work. In order for money spells to work, you need to supplement it with effort on your part.

If you want to invite wealth into your home...

This spell makes your home more receptive to prosperity.

- The first step is to sprinkle some sandalwood chips underneath the doormat of your house's main door. Then, add dried basil leaves and patchouli.

- Next, set a silver coin on the center above the herbs.

- Return the mat to its normal place.

- Afterwards, position yourself so that you are facing the north. Stand on the doormat.

- Recite a heartfelt incantation inviting wealth into your home. Ask for prosperity and new opportunities to find their way to your doorstep.

- You may seek the help of deities related to abundance (ex. Fortuna, Lakshmi)

If you want to attract moneymaking opportunities wherever you go…

This Wiccan money spell involves creating a charm which you may carry with you to help you attract new financial opportunities. Take note that you may only begin this spell on a Thursday.

- Obtain a silver bowl and add a few broken up cinnamon sticks. Then, throw in some patchouli and dill. Add also a few drops of pine oil.

- Then, place a Malachite crystal in the bowl and bury it beneath the mixture.

- Cover the silver bowl. It is to remain untouched for seven days.

- On the seventh day, retrieve the Malachite.

- Place the crystal in your pocket.

- If you have an altar at home devoted to your patron deity, set the silver bowl there. Otherwise, keep it in a clean and safe place.

If you want to increase your existing wealth…

This spell will involve honoring your gods/goddesses of abundance and is to be performed during a waxing moon.

- First you'll need to set up an altar in a room which will provide you quick access to a door leading outside.

- The altar should be situated in the east side of your circle. It should have white candles that are coated in sandalwood oil.

- There should also be one green candle previously anointed with pine oil.

- Also to be included is an orange candle covered with basil oil.

- On the altar should be four *old* coins.

- You will also need pine incense.

- Light the white candles and the green candle, as well as the pine incense.

- Obtain a handful of sweet basil and pass it over the white candles, the green candle, and finally, the pine incense. This is to be done three times.

- Afterwards, scatter the sweet basil around the green candle.

- Obtain a new coin and clutch it in your hand.

- Circle the altar in a clockwise direction and utter an incantation invoking your god/goddess of abundance to bring to you what you see. By this, you are referring to the symbols of wealth in your altar.

- Spin around rapidly in a clockwise direction.

- Then, go outside the room. Once outdoors, toss the new coin that you are holding in your hand.

- Observe where the new coin lands. This is where you must bury it along with the four old coins.

- While doing this, offer the money to your deity and beseech his/her generosity.

Example:

"Hecate, I offer money to thee...

Send prosperity to me.

Five coins I give thee,

Return it times three.

Such is my will.

So mote it be."

- After the incantation, go back to where your altar is and extinguish the candles.

- After seven days, return with a green pouch (preferably silk) to store your talisman. Also, bring with you a chalice with saltwater and fresh pine incense to burn.

- Light the virgin candle (the orange one).

- In your mind's eye, envision wealth going inside your altar.

- Then, retrieve the coins from the ground and bring them back to your altar. There, cleanse your coins with saltwater in the chalice.

- Pass the coins over the smoke emanating from pine incense, and the orange candle.

- Then, one by one, place the coins in the green silk pouch. Put in the new coin last.

- Afterwards, arrange nine grains of rock salt around the opening of the silk pouch.

- Position yourself so that you are facing in the eastward direction.

- Once again, invoke the power of your god/goddess through an incantation. Also, ask for the aid of the elements: the earth, fire, air, and water.

- Pin the green talisman pouch inside your garments. This is to be worn every day for one week. At night, you may lay the pouch on the altar where you are to visualize your intent before going to bed.

- Then, after a week, you may keep your talisman pouch in the eastern part of your home.

If you want to banish your debts...

Perform this spell under a waning moon.

- Light any incense of your choice.

- Then, obtain a purple candle and anoint it with any oil you prefer. Sandalwood, bergamot, and clove are among the most popular oils for prosperity.

- On a parchment paper that's about 6 centimeters in width, write down all of your debts. Use black ink.

- When you're done, draw a banishing pentagram on the back of the paper. To draw a banishing pentagram, begin the star at the lower left point, moving up to the top point and finally ending again in the lower left point.

- On the purple candle, carve another banishing pentagram with the use of a burin (engraving tool) or a pin.

- Afterwards, roll the parchment and place it in a candle holder. Next, secure the candle on top of it.

- Concentrate on the different ways in which you can solve your debt problems. Is it possible for you to obtain a new job? To cut down your expenses? Are you expecting a new financial opportunity to come your way? Focus on that.

- Now, in your mind's eye, visualize yourself and imagine that you are free from all your debts. Allow the joy to fill you.

- Then, light the candle.

- After that, take it to the east direction and seek the help of the Spirit of Air.

(Ex. "Spirit of air, I beseech thee. Acknowledge my intent to be debt-free.")

- Then, place the candle back into the holder and allow it to burn to the end. Eventually, the paper with your debts will catch fire. The burning will symbolize the clearing of your debts.

- In your mind's eye, watch your debts as they are one by one replaced by wealth.

Note that after performing this spell, your debts will not just miraculously disappear. Instead, a solution which will help you in paying your debts will come your way. This may be in the form of an unexpected fortune, an opportunity for a side job, or a bright idea which will help you make/save money.

Even before the spell takes effect, you are bound by honor to avoid creating further debts.

Chapter 13: Spells for Success

Success for different individuals bears different faces. To some, success is synonymous to wealth. To others, success means obtaining fame and power. Meanwhile, there are some people who consider themselves successful when they've reached their goals for health or happiness.

If you want to obtain your dream job…

This spell is to be performed during the night of the New Moon. Candle spells work wonderfully well with success spells because fire signifies drive.

- Begin by lighting some cinnamon incense.

- Obtain a green candle which will symbolize prosperity. Obtain two brown candles which will symbolize the career position that you are aspiring for. Lastly, obtain one candle which will symbolize you. For this, you may want to choose your zodiac color.

- Using bergamot oil, coat all of the candles from one end to another. As previously mentioned, bergamot is one of the herbs linked with abundance.

- Cast a circle. Invite your god/goddess of prosperity to enter your circle.

- The brown candles must be placed in the middle of your circle. Meanwhile, the green candle should be set on the right side. The candle which symbolizes you should be set on the left side.

- Light the candle representing you. While doing this, chant an invocation asking the god/goddess to help smooth your way to success.

(Ex.: "Horus, God of Success, open the way to me. Provide me with a chance. For such is my given right...")

- Then, light the green candle. Utter the words: "Success is mine." and believe it with all of your heart.

- Lastly, light the two candles which symbolize your dream job. In your mind's eye, envision yourself achieving your goal, not immediately, but step by step. Then, think of how it would feel once you are finally able to get the job of your dreams. Allow that joyful sensation to fill your soul.

- Utter these words: "As I view this in my mind, so it must be."

- Put out the candles. You will need to relight the brown ones every night. Allow them to burn for 9 minutes. This is also how long you will perform your nightly visualization of your goals.

If you want to invite success into your life...

This Moon Spell is to be performed at 8:00 in the evening.

- Cast a circle and light a golden candle. Invite the Moon Goddess (Luna, Artemis, Selene, or whichever deity you regard as the Goddess of the Moon) to grace your circle with her presence.

- You should be holding an image in your hand that represents what success is to you. It could be a person, a place, or an object. It can be something that you've made or a proof of your past achievements.

- Empower your chosen symbol through a personal incantation calling upon the Moon Goddess's help to bless, with her divine powers of success, the picture that you are holding.

- Then say: "In the name of the Divine Goddess of the Moon, so mote it be!"

- Place the image near the candlelight and then take several deep breaths. Imagine that with each inhalation, you are pulling in success. With each exhalation, envision the fear, insecurities, and other negative emotions leaving your body.

- Lastly, close your circle by thanking the goddess.

- Keep the image symbolizing success on your altar, or put it in any sacred spot in your home.

Chapter 14:
Spells for Happiness

Like success, happiness may mean different things to various individuals. For this reason, this chapter will focus on basic spells for happiness and those for overcoming depression.

If you want to invite happiness into your life...

- Obtain three candles for this spell. You may go with either yellow or orange candles. Either way, all three candles should be of the same color.

- Anoint the three candles with cedar oil. Afterwards, set them on your altar.

- Light the candles. While doing this, sprinkle some rosemary and marjoram around them.

- Focus on the heat emanating from the candle flames. Allow that warmth to fill you.

- Then, with a personal chant, invite happiness into your life.

    Example:

    "I am happy.

    I am free.

    Negativity dwells not within me."

- Afterwards, hold your hands over the candle flames and once again, absorb that warm happy glow. Be careful when doing this. Then, envision that warmth filling your body, flowing from your hands, your arms, and all the way to your heart.

- Think of positive thoughts. At this point, there should be no room for negative thinking in your head.

- Leave the candles to burn to the end.

If you wish to overcome depression...

Prior to performing the spell, select a safe and quiet venue which will enable you to focus deeply.

- Draw a circle.

- Tie a black-colored strip of cloth around your wrist.

- Then, light a black candle. While doing this, you need to bring yourself to admit that at the moment, your soul is filled with darkness. Nevertheless, you shall banish these dark thoughts through the power of fire.

- Afterwards, with the flame from your black candle, light a new candle. This time, the candle should be pure white.

- Fill a bowl halfway with earth. Then, fill the rest of the bowl with rainwater. The earth, in its blackness, signifies the powers of the dark. The water, in its purity, signifies the light powers. You need both the light and the dark in order to heal. For the light cannot exist without the dark, and vice versa.

- With the use of a feather tip, mix the water and earth mixture in the bowl. Continue doing this until the two elements are completely combined.

- Say these words: "I am doing this so that I may free my soul."

- The soil in the bowl is now moist. Dip the tip of the feather into it and use it to draw a banishing pentagram on a piece of paper.

- Afterwards, remove the black strip from your wrist. Roll the paper and tie the black ribbon around it. By doing this, you are binding the curse. Mention this in your incantation.

- Extinguish the candles.

- Dig a hole in the ground in which you will bury the paper. Mark the site because you will have to return after a week.

- For seven consecutive nights, you need to utter a personal incantation. Include this in your chant: "I can feel that my soul is light. I can feel that it is bright. I can feel that it is free."

- On the evening of the seventh day, retrieve the scroll from the earth and remove the black strip.

- After that, burn the paper along with your feelings of depression.

Then speak these words out loud: "I am free. The darkness has fled from my soul. From now on, I swear to dwell only in the light."

Chapter 15:
Spells for Healing

If you want to heal yourself...

- For this particular spell, you'll be using a current photo of yourself.

- Arrange six candles in a circle around your image. Three of these candles should be purple while the other three should be blue.

- Empower each candle by invoking the spirit of the elements. For instance, concentrate on one candle and utter these words: "I empower thee with the Spirit of Fire..." Then, turn your focus on the candle beside it and speak: "I empower thee with the Spirit of Earth..."

- Beseech the powers of the elements: Earth, Water, Air, and Fire to cure you from your disease, be it physical, mental, emotional, or spiritual.

- Then, light all of the candles. While doing this, ask the Spirit of the Elements to consume your disease and your pain in flames.

- Close the spell by uttering these words: "Freedom shall be mine. For such is my will."

- Perform this spell for several succeeding nights. Do this until you are completely free from your illness.

If you want to heal others…

- Light three candles. They should all be white.

- Then, in a big glass jar, keep a photograph of the person that you would like to help. While doing this, say the subject's full name out loud.

- Add brightly colored flower petals inside the jar. Any kind of blossom will do as long as it is fresh.

- While adding the different ingredients, explain why you are doing so. For example, say this out loud: "To this jar, I add brightly colored petals to bring you joy and energy."

- Instill a few drops of rose oil into the jar. You may say these words or something similar to them: "To this jar, I add rose oil to soothe thy pain." Make your incantation personal.

- Instill a few drops of water into the jar, preferably from a natural free-flowing source. You may say these words: "To this jar, I add water to symbolize life."

- Then, proclaim this out loud: "Make (name of the sick person) healthy once again. For the right to life is his/her given gift."

- You may choose to bring this healing jar outside a hospital where the person is confined. Alternatively, you may put it outside their house.

If you want to heal someone who's far away…

- On an onion, engrave the name of the person whom you would like to help.

- If you have a garden, you may plant the onion bulb there. If you don't, you may make use of a pot.

- Now, you need to place various objects of magick in each direction of your house. To invoke the power of the North, bury a stone there. To invoke the power of the East, bury a white feather there. To invoke the power of the South, dig a hole in that area and add three drops of rosemary oil. To invoke the power of the West, bury a shell, preferably a white colored one, in that place.

- The last magickal object is the horseshoe which you will need to lay on the area where you've planted the bulb. As you put it there, beseech the help of the God of War for this battle between sickness and health.

Conclusion

Thank you again for downloading this book!

I hope this book was able to help you learn more about Wicca and its spells!

The next step is to put this information to use, and begin practicing Wicca and performing Wiccan spells and rituals!

Finally, if you enjoyed this book, please take the time to share your thoughts and post a review on Amazon. It'd be greatly appreciated!

Thank you and good luck!

www.ingramcontent.com/pod-product-compliance
Lightning Source LLC
LaVergne TN
LVHW021736060526
838200LV00052B/3299